Why So Blue?

To Great Auntie Fern,
Sending so much
love

For
the lost souls
& the broken hearted

This book is a compilation of art and poetry, focusing on emotion, youth and growth.

Contents

The Lonely...1

The Love...63

The End...97

The Lonely

Suburbia

It seems like the whole world is being consumed
The youth are all zombies and will soon be in tombs
It is not just the toxic fumes
Yet the future is what we consume
There was a time where we were social and keen
Now we all obey a screen
Oh no!
You do not validate me!
I must pay a small fee?
To stay in this bubble
Yet now I want out
Pop it!
Now set me free!
The stars used to light up the night
Now it is just a window
Is this all our kids will know?
Maybe I am just a palm tree in the snow in Suburbia

The Glow

We live for the glow
It illuminates the darkness
And lifts our self esteem
Yet we should not live for the glow
For as we all should know
It can take its toll
And grasp control

Waste

What else is there to do than waste time away
Clicking and clicking each tab day by day
To amuse our mind for a short period of time
No more toys or trees to climb
Just a screen to stare into

Red Solo Cup

A packed full room of lost souls
Getting wasted on cheap beer
Just to talk to one another without fear
The emotion poured into their red solo cup
Boys told to beef up
Girls told to clean up
For me I am fed up
I refuse to drown in my red solo cup

Ordinary People

Ordinary people walk along a road
A road with only one direction
They long for and seek perfection
With a lover's affection

Ordinary people walk side by side
Working day and night just to get by

Work all day makes a diamond dull
Work all day makes a star burn out
You've left a poet's hand cramped
And a singer's mouth dry

Where did my inspiration go?
Where did my ambition go?
I guess it is true
Life is just easier following the same road

Gods And Monsters

We live in a land
It is fantasy to the common man
The kingdom set out a wicked plan
To not trust someone or hold their hand
For we walk among gods and monsters
Some conceal who they are behind a mask
Some give up
Reject who they are as they sip through a flask
A question I'll always ask
Why is our land full of gods and monsters?

The Game

Are you really a winner?
Or just a silent sinner?
Are you really a loser?
Or just a loud abuser?
We all enter a game
With the intent to blame
For we rather frame
Then own up to the action
For the game is a test
A crazy abstraction
To see if your intent is golden
The rules you uphold in
The game is a test to see if you are a player
Or if your motive is to win as your conscience
grows grayer
For the game is not about success
It is really to confess
If you are ready to roll the die

Original

Scroll, click, copy, paste

What happened
It seems like the world has gone mad
Or maybe just lazy
Either way it has eaten my brain raw
For no one creates anymore
We just copy
Something nice for us to see
Then hoping we'll never get caught
Without even giving it a thought
We just

Scroll, click, copy, paste

Concrete City

Somedays I wonder
If the skies are always full of thunder
If the sky only cries in april
If beyond the clouds the sun is alright
For now it is out of sight
I look above the tall buildings to reach the sun
Yet the concrete swallows it whole

To/Too/Two & One

Us & them.
Right & wrong.
Yes & no.
Jekyll & Hyde.
We all pick a side.
We pave a road.
We write a bill.
We all want an answer.
Just one,
Not two.
Yet there is nothing but sides to choose.

American Dream

You had it all
Only to fall
The "American Dream"
So it seemed
It was not what you wanted
You'd whimper
You'd weep
But at least you had somewhere to sleep
To greedy to give
Only you would keep
But today you cry
You've lost it all
Deep regret and sadness you feel
At this moment you'd die for a meal
So next time you say
"I want this so bad"
Think of someone who would love
What you have

We are a Rainbow

Dreamcast
Technicolour
Like no other
We are the rainbow connection
That special selection
Each colour is vital
For you to find your title

On Fleek

Culture
It's weird
It's always changing
I don't understand it
But something that has never changed is the
Beauty standard
It makes me sick
For a women to feel lesser
While their eyes are locked on their dresser
Just to fit into the trend
They have scars that a lipstick can't mend
Millions of photographs posted and sent
As a young girl I didn't understand
What this meant
For I despise a phrase
That is being used these days
Just another reason for our generation
To throw shade
"On Fleek" is a phrase praised by our
Decade

Vogue

It's true
No matter the issue
I feel like a whale
Am I a women or have I failed?
For are these women in the magazines
As pretty as they seem?
They are radient
They beam
But it is a mere illusion
They cough up blood
Bathe in mud
To be beautiful
But in the end those very starlets
Receive more issues than Vogue

Breathe in the Air

Look at you
Focusing on everything you do
Subconsciencly forgetting the other
Let it be
Maybe then you will see
Yet you continue to parish
Under your own eyes
Using your own demise

People Pleaser

EVERYONE is against you.
EVERYONE watches everything you do.
EVERYONE tilts their head when they look at you.
EVERYONE is concerned with what you do.
EVERYONE cares.
What a silly thought process.
How is everyone supposed to care about you
If they are caught up in themselves.

The Lost Search

Admit it
You failed
And it is okay
See, perfection is a lost search
You will never find it
It has gone extinct
When you seek perfection
A little piece of you dies
And everywhere you go you will see lies
Telling you how to feel
Lulling you to think
It will make you look skinner
And that it will make you whole
But all it will do is just leave you empty
So you will crave more as you starve

Stuck in a Puzzle

This is a picture of a puzzled young girl
Here she was trying
Trying to impress
Tending to overdress to mask her insecurities
This is a picture of a puzzled young girl
Who shared her love with the wrong people
Their toxicity broke her heart into pieces
When she managed to pick them up
She put the puzzle back together
This time she saw a different picture

Barbie

So you want to be a Barbie?
Made of plastic
Your heart so elastic
So you want to be someone's toy?
Have no idenitiy
Other then belonging to a boy
He the provider of your counterfiet joy
So you wanna look good?
Contributer to the machine
Where you look the way you should
You follow someone else's footprints which
Have already been stood
Go ahead and be a Barbie
But suddenly when you peer into the mirror
And no longer like what you see
No one will feel sympathy

Violent Eyes

I couldn't care less what people think of me
Because judgemental people are insecure
They prey on their victims
From their eyes you see violence
And they keep their silence
They have nothing better to do
Than point out flaws
Without seeing the mark left behind by their claws
But then again
When they look in the mirror
They feel insecure
For those same eyes
Are staring right back in their reflection

18

Hazy mind
Bright eyes
A kind of darkness words cannot describe
A grim October day
A wide smile
Full of rotten decay
Eighteen
Alone in the great big world
What is there to do but cry?
Kiss seventeen goodbye..

Screaming Soul

I was betrayed by the ones I loved most
I didn't understand the state I was in
Tired of riding a dream
That was further than it seemed
I want to live happy
But I have nothing to sacrifice
Other then my artistic soul
It is screaming for me to listen
But I only hear whispers
This frustration made me cold
Colder than a winters night
Angry for I couldn't be who I wanted to be
I was trying to stay sane
But I cracked
Just a floor tile repeatedly getting stepped on
As my dreams shattered in front of my very eyes
By the ones I loved most

Arctic

I am as cold as the Arctic
I am as sharp as an iceberg
But I bathe in the sun
Hoping to melt away my flaws
To no surprise the sun went to hideaway
Leaving the sky cloudy and gray
Is it fate?
Is there a gate?
For I am frozen solid
I shiver under each dark cloud
I cannot move until I am a perfect cube
Slowly I will try to dig away
At my flaws so deeply solid

Cold Blood

My blood has run cold
Since I was seven years old
Never understood
Nor fit into a mold
Never listened or did what I was told
But my cold blood is what made me fearless
And bold

Correct

Congrats!
You are correct
The illness will take effect
It will spread to your mind body and soul
I am not a fire you cannot warm me with coal

The Pill

Is it true that with a single pill
It will make me less ill?
For I feel like it has stripped much more than
My crazy
I am an old wall my paint peeling
To show my old pattern
But all the pill did was paint me a new colour

Smoke

So beautifully distant
Blowing in the wind
Fading away into the air
How I imagine a soul disappears
Once we are dead
How thoughts drift around in ones head
Like smoke one day
I'll fade away

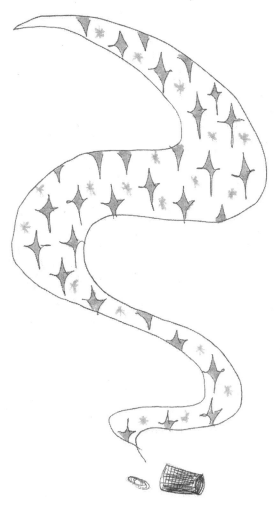

Claw the Ice

Frozen under a thick layer of Ice
Yet able to swim free
As cold as I can be
Under the sea
Yet to be frozen
Hidden away
Is not how I plan to spend the rest of my days

Blue Neighbourhood

Something about the night sky that
Made me Feel curious
Something about the stars that
Made me feel hopeful
Something about the city screams my name
Something about the youth and our new
Found fame
The wild dreamers looking for inspiration
The young love locked away
In a blue neighbourhood

Clouds

Hand on my heart
I start the journey
Head held high
I walk along the path
As rain trickled down
My grin became a frown
My blue skies
Became crying eyes
I reach for my red hood
As the trees over grow the path
It was my only map
Unfortunately now I was trapped
This misfortune similar to a fairytale
Reminded me of a sharp tooth beast
Who would soon appear
As I clutch on to my hood so dear
The wind lifted me off my feet
As I saw the trees grow smaller beneath
I was blown into the clouds
Where I secretly always was

Space

I look to Space
Wishing my existance on earth I could erase
For I wish to be reborn
My life a notebook constantly being torn
Take me to Space
The Solar System I must face
Let a planet choose me

Tears

The taste of salty tears
As she talked about her fears
Under satin sheets
She was knee deep
It was a murky sea
It was not a place she should be
But a series of events caused her to trip
Her centre of balance began to tip
The tears started just as a puddle and now
Form an ocean
She reached for a potion
An elixir
Something to make her feel better
To cure her strange weather

Misfit

I am clay
I just mold
Just something for someone to hold
But I crave something sweet not bitter
Maybe if I were blonde and fitter?
Maybe if I wore a dress made of glitter?
I could fit in somewhere
I could feel free to be myself
Yet I guess that's too easy and unfair
And who would generally care
Care enough to know the person I want to be
Must I get on one knee?
I shall beg for belonging
For now I am a misfit

Judgement

Your eyes pierce through my skin
Like a sharp blade
I feel my vibrant soul rapidly fade
For lately I need validation
In this self obsessed nation
So I leave my doors open for your opinion
As the people swarm like minions
For there was a villain
But he was not real
He was just sitting in my brain chilling
Soaking the thrill in
For when I question
He takes the pen to fill in
But the confidence I lack
Has put my soul under attack
And just a matter of fact
When I begin to wonder
The villain grabs his bags and begins to pack

The Ranking

At one point I wanted to have it all
So every step I took would keep me from a fall
I was just a 1 and wanted to be a 5
For I thought it would make me feel alive
I wanted success so I could thrive
But as I watched my dreams take a tumble
I realized I was no longer genuine or humble
I just wanted to fit into the mold
I would do anything I was told
To get a higher ranking

Caught up in my Tea

My nose pressed upon a dirty old textbook
As I hear the girls giggle
Yet I was not interested not even a little
I couldn't sit still I'd move around and fiddle
As I pack up my bag
I spy a tea cup in the corner of my eye
Maybe one sip I will just try
Maybe it will give me wings
Maybe I will fly
Maybe I will not be as shy
To my delight
The cup was in sight
I had transformed
I was reborn
A change had arose
I now had the urge to brag and boast
For I was not interested in toast
Just tea
At sixteen
I was caught up in my tea

Aliens

No one knows me
Yet I watch them stare
Was I that mean that I turned green?
For I feel like an alien in this place
Yet I've never been to outer space
But truthfully I would not mind seeing the stars

Paper Bag

I wore a paper bag
Through the day and night
I was afraid to show who I really was
What was stuck and lurking inside my head
But my brain was hungry and had hardly
Been fed
So please help me burn this paper bag

Savages

Noisy hallways
Clouded vision
No glasses could assist the permanent damage
When the savages came and attacked me
And the person I wanted to be

Release

I felt release
I was no longer among
Old hallways
Ripped books
Dated uniforms
Judgmental eyes
Insecure minds
& horrible memories which still haunt me

Comfortably Numb

A faded desire
With an active mind
Tumbled into wet concrete
Now I was stuck
Movement helped my eggshell soul
From cracking so often
It gave me a direction
Somewhere to go
Yet now my body does not know
It was like my brain had reprogrammed
To opposite day
And wouldn't listen to what I would say
I lay by the window
Wrapped up in my doubt
Looking beyond a white picket fence

Sad

I was sad
And it made me mad
This fear is very clear
This rage is centre stage
This hole which I have fallen down
Is very deep
This love which I have is quite cheap
This very day I sit and weep
The next day I'll sit in the dark and sleep
This mountain I am trying to climb
Is awfully steep
So here I lay
Ready to decay
Please someone take me away

Isolation

Isolation
I do not recommend it
It will destroy you
Every thought exaggerated
Every dream far away on a winding road
Every feeling as deep as a canyon
I am so immersed
If I jump it will make no difference
My eyes flow like waterfalls
And collect into a salty ocean
I swim in a pit of emotion
And when I think I have reached the bottom
I begin gasping for air
I would yell and pled why it is not fair
For I was almost there

Ringtone

It made me sad
When I did not hear a familiar sound
When I looked down
I would stare at a blank screen and frown
For where did my friends go
I guess I'll never know

In my Bedroom

Alone to myself
No one to bother me
Locked away from reality
In my bedroom
Crazy how my mind could get lost for hours
Through windy storms and April showers
In my bedroom
I say I'm never lonely
Because of my virtual reality
But slowly it is killing me
In my bedroom

Webs

I made a web
To catch a friend
Who would stay with me until the very end
Someone who could see
I was not broken
Just bent
There was no "whole"
Just a dent
With all my energy I spent
Making this web I grew tired
I am not a hard drive
I am not wired
But other peoples' lives I would admire
Wondering what I must acquire...
To have a friend
You cannot build webs
For the wind could blow them away

Dimmed Horizons

I used to think every morning
The sun would peek through the cloudy skies
Yet time after time
The clouds seem to overpower
The sharp yellow rays
It is an unpleasant feeling I have day after day
Similar to when you mix two vibrant colours
Yet it produces a dark gray
Similar to my heart which easily cracks
Like dried clay
Similar to an unloved animal
That has gone astray
So here in the bed I lay
Watching a dimmed horizon
Hoping for the sun to shine through

Around the World

I wonder if I am the only one
Who feels this way
On a cold floor as I lay
I wonder if around the world so large
I connect with someone
And let my brain charge

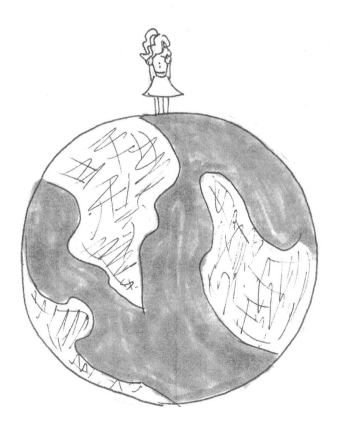

Key

I am only a number in this cage
No plot to my story just a blank page
Now orange was the colour of my attire
There was no promotion in this cage
Anyway of getting higher
There was a burning desire in each numbers
Heart starting a mass fire
But it was useless to get enraged
For this cage was only a phase
In four years the key will unlock my cage

The Desert

I am all alone in the desert
I am a prick but I am not a cactus
I am thirsty but I prefer love
I am wet but in dry land
I don't get along with anyone
For I drain out all the fun
So here I stand all alone in the desert

Train of Thought

There it goes again leaving the station
Not even giving me a warning
I have a paper due in the morning
Yet I watched the train pass by
It had no breaks
As I stare at my screen
My eyes start to ache
I just wanna finish the sentence
Sadly my train already derailed
I was out of luck
Should have bought a damn schedule

I am Restless

How dare I question my faint?
Why don't I pour a cup of tea and wait?
The truth is my roots will always stay the same
Although my petals may change
Life is a constant puzzle
That gets rearranged

Seeds

Nothing can grow without a seed
It is what they all need
There is a journey each follows to bloom
Not all are the same
As you would assume

Rain

Teardrops are like rain
Once the storm is over
It's like a large weight has been lifted
I love rain yet tears make feel weak
And only happiness is what I seek
Yet life does not work like that
It's important to have stormy skies in order
To see a rainbow

Mother Nature

I was a river
My flow a fast pace
Through all the wind I would face
I enjoyed the life which surrounded me
Vibrant flowers which stood snug by my side
But in the winter they would hide
They shrivelled up and died
Yet my motion continued under
A thick layer of ice
After a frigid winter
I thought that Mother Nature
Would continue her pattern
Yet her presence drifted away
As my river started to shrink
I was alarmed
Didn't know what to think
I was now part of a dryland
Here water is sealed away in cans
I couldn't move
I was stuck
I was thirsty...

But Mother was no longer near
This isolation then brought fear
I am a desert
I will wait for the rain
People may call me insane
But why would I care
If they stop and stare
Just because I am stuck
Doesn't mean I can't dream

Soap

In a puddle I lay
Waiting for the day to waste away
Wash my slate clean
Take away my sin
So my new era can being
For all you need is a little soap

Blue 2.0

I want to be myself but the 2.0
In the trash is my soul I would throw
I want to be reborn
I want to glow
Mold me into something new with dough

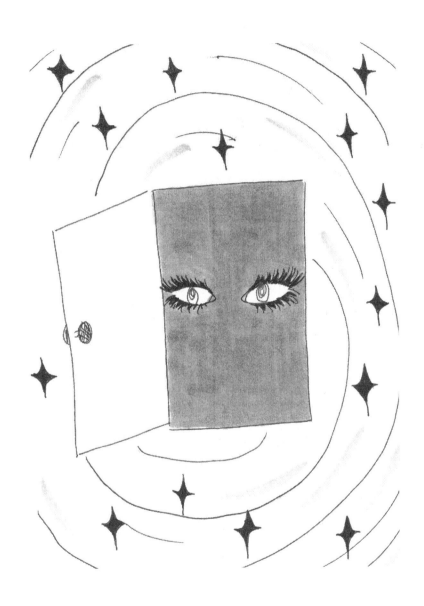

Questions

Nothing is how it seems
So I question everything
Even my dreams
I'm stuck in a time warp
Where everything stays the same
A daily dose of reality fills my veins
It came to a part where my brain
Started to drain
Until I realized it was all an illusion
A delusion
With no conclusion
For I held a key to unlock the next door
Even though there was another floor
So I ask myself
What am I waiting for?
My brain full of confusion
I didn't want to make an intrusion

The Love

Crushed

He walks into the room
My heart fell
A sudden doom
For his eyes a shade of blue
Made my heart bloom
I was ready to be juiced
I was his type of fruit
But to my surprise
As the whites of his eyes grew small
I felt a warm tear on my cheek begin to fall
For he didn't like me at all

Matchbox

I was stuck in the darkness
I was hungry for the light
But I grew tired
Gave up the fight
Then he came along and brought the light
He held a single match from a matchbox
He was radiant witty knocked me off my socks
I accidentally bumped the box from his grasp
His eyes grew large as he gasped
All he had was that one match in his hand
There was nothing else to offer
I am left in the dark

Burn Out

Let me be a star
For I have come so far
I am tired of sitting around
Twiddling my thumbs
For I long to be your number one

Take Out

What am I to you
Just a light snack or a full feast?
For you pick me apart piece by piece
You pick away straight to the bone
Only after the moon rise
You would answer the phone
Although I am tender
I am not a takeout meal

Once Upon A Time

A forbidden desire
Reminds me of an old fairytale
With a prince and a maiden with skin so pale
Searching for an elated feeling in a dark time
When it is still worth it including
A steep mountain to climb
I have never lived where love was a voyage
Or where there was a lavish family so royal
As peculiar as it may seem
This is a feeling I still dream

An Artist

Dab a little colour on my cheeks
Nothing a little colour would not fix
It is not an elixir
A drink you can mix
I am one of a kind

Cherry Soda

He liked cherry soda
He liked a tall glass
He liked the way it would glide down
His throat
His tongue full of flavour the drink would coat
But he failed to realize his unhealthy obsession

Polly Pocket

I am not your toy
Even though you are just a boy
I am not your dolly
You cannot call me Polly
I am not made for your pocket

Tangled

She is in knots
Tied up to the wrong man
Although she knows his flaws
Like the back of her hand
Why can't you see the dark cloud
Covering the sun
Why can't you realize what he has done
Everything is broken
My words left unspoken
You tell me to stay calm
Even when he drops a bomb

Fear in her Eyes

She wore a black dress
To mourn her memories
She did not want to remember him
He threw her in the ocean
When she could not swim
Then she realized the trouble she was in
For there was fear in her eyes

Pure

Why is it so hard for white to stay clean?
It has been this way for many since the age of 17
Weird how your perception
Would suddenly change
Making your morals rearrange
So I would soak for a little while
Hotlines Helplines I'd dial
For shame clouded my mind body and soul
Wish I was no longer stained
It has drained blood from my brain
My god I've gone completely insane
What has gone wrong?
I've been looking for a cure
But then I realized it is not the end of the world
Not to be pure

The Man and the Monster

He was consumed by a nightmare
He was no longer a teddybear
He plucked me like a sweet pear
When I look in his eyes I see a monster
My heart he would slaughter
My cup full of water and he was only thirsty

Sour

He was sour
Each and every hour
Every time he saw my face he would frown
Maybe it was because I stole his crown
I dethroned the king from feeling mighty
Neither a king nor god
While I was his Aphrodite
He demands power
And now he is sour

Boiling Blood

Every time I see your face it sends a fire sensation
Throughout my body
I once trusted someone so dear
Someone who could make me feel bright
And dry a tear
Yet you left me on high temperatures
You would watch my blood boil
You let out a sinister smile
Your lungs filled with a scent so vile
So I burned you back
Singed your finger tips
So you could no longer touch me with your lips

Outrage

How could you be this way?
You broke that item are you going to pay?
Because lately it seems day to day
That you do not care anymore
It started on a sad day in May
I was weak, you smoking a jay
There are pros and cons I would weigh
I read back my words page by page
It fills my soul with rage
I was just another step on your stairs
To reach a higher step with your peers
Now I dry my own tears
They were all in outrage
About how she "changed"

Envy

I hate this part
I'm not sure where it start
Wishing he and you were apart
For I guess I am full of envy
I hate the way he looks at you
How you are perfect at everything you do
Wish I could be like you too
If you only knew
I guess I am full of envy
Wish I could just be happy with me
Truly want to just be the best I can be
But I am full of envy

Paint

I asked you to mix it
Mix the paint
It is too thick
We cannot make art with goop
Yet you did not listen to me
Instead went on your own spree
Made your own recipe
You added water but that made the paint
Too runny
I tried to fix your combination
But the damage was already done
I could not let go for that room stood bare
It was not fair
I could not use the paint
It was tainted
The fumes were toxic

Glass

I am easily cracked
I do not do well under pressure
Even if it is a small fracture
My glass is weak
A strong layer I seek
So when you fill me up I will not leak

Scissors

I always kept scissors on me
Sometimes when you need something dearly
It is sealed shut
Sometimes if you try by yourself
You will get cut
They were handy for a while
Until they started to get out of hand
Scissors may be helpful but are dangerous
If you depend on them and keep them
By your side

Dirty Laundry

I stuck with you through the strange weather
I would hold you close keep you warm
Then suddenly I was thrown into a pile
With other used items
To be washed and then used again
It hurts as I tumble round and round
Spinning fast upside down
Sadly he did not read the label
I was to be hand washed
Yet he did not care
For once I shrunk
I was worthless
No longer belonging to him
Just the trash bin

Loose Change

Don't you forget about me
As I lay in your cool pocket
Waiting patiently until I am wanted
But I am barely desired
I am a penny
Worthless to the common soul
I rather you throw me away
Then hold me tight by your side
In your very pocket

My Heart

My heart is a wild creature
My ribs are the cage
Keeping my heart from leaping
Instead it is locked away sleeping
If my heart were wild
I might have been a lost child
Broken from the start
You would pull each string from my heart

Cigarette

You burned a hole through my heart
This must have been where the trouble
Would start
I hold tight to your hand
As you light me up like a cigarette
Then you throw me away
Once I've been used
And you
Hold me close and press your lips
Toward me
Why do you hold me like you do..
Then go on to your next one

Affection/Connection

When it comes to affection
You will face rejection
There will be someone with an objection
Someone there to make a correction
Another trying to point you in a
Different direction
Someone disappointed
When obsessed with perfection
Another with arms open wide in protection
Someone to integrate
To make an inspection
But only you will know if you have
A connection

Polaroid

Print me out
Mix around my colours
Edit out my flaws
Make me the perfect polaroid photograph

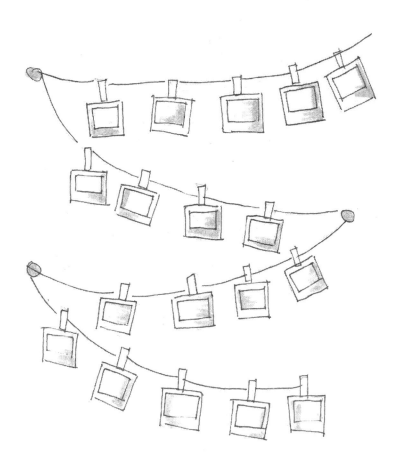

Fast Fashion

I am designer
I am like no other
You may pay millions if you wish
Yet that will not make you happier
I am a Versace dress
The only thing I will do is leave your closet
A mess
Don't worry about me
For sure I will be
Out of style next month

Repair

There will always be someone to push you
When you are down
There will always be someone
Who looks at you with a frown
There will always be someone
Who loves to hate
There will always be someone
Who drops a heavy weight
There will always be someone
Who is screaming for love
While they stay mute
Who will continue to dispute
Until they realize
Beyond cloudy skies
Beyond wicked lies
Beyond broken ties
Beyond your blue eyes
There is room to repair

Paper

Paper gives me somewhere to pour
Clusters of letters
Paper allows me to express emotion
And feel better
Yet paper is fragile
It can be torn
It can be burned
It can be soaked by a sudden storm
I watch the ink thebleed
Paper is like trust
It can get crumpled
Even with an effort to repair
It will never be perfect again

Drip Drop

I poured my heart all over you
You made me feel electric
Brand new
Wondering if you had the same
Feelings too
My heart dropped and shattered
When you told me
You wished to be clean
While I poured my heart all over you

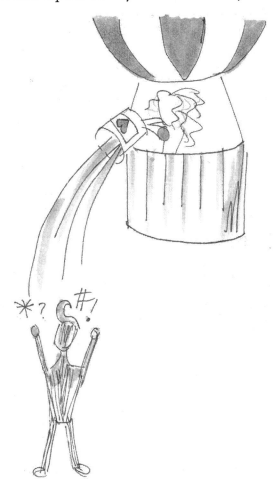

Ashes

You burnt me to the bone
You captured my soul and spirit
With the flames
Ironic how you prayed for peace
Yet took out your rage on me
I am a blank page
You were an artist full of life
But you would rather smoke all day
Leave me to rot and decay
As you put me in your tray
Along with your other ashes

Yours

I cannot lie to myself anymore
I am so close to walking out the door
I thought we were something special for sure
Yet you ate me whole like an apple
Straight to the core
Now I feel my brain melting straight
To the floor
It looked like a murder scene complete
With guts, blood and gore
I thought I was your top drawer
But for you
I was just another score
All I wanted was to be yours

The End

Little Blue

It is true I am a Little Blue
Thought one day it would go away as I grew
Just like the sea and sky I drew
Just like an early morning dew
I was indeed a little blue
For a while I did not mind the hue
The skies seemed like a good view
But then it became clear that it was stuck to me
Like glue
Being blue consumed me whole
My mentality grew weak and it took a toll
Now I do not want to be blue
Please someone make me new
But something I never knew or realized
Was in order to find true happiness you have to
Be a Little Blue

Blue city
Blue neighbourhood
Blue parents
Blue freinds
Contributed to making me Little Blue
Yet there is a spectrum still to discover.

Thank you.
Much Love.

Made in the USA
Middletown, DE
17 May 2017